Chemical and Biological Warfare

Chemical and Biological Warfare
The Cruelest Weapons

Revised Edition

Laurence Pringle

Enslow Publishers, Inc.

40 Industrial Road	PO Box 38
Box 398	Aldershot
Berkeley Heights, NJ 07922	Hants GU12 6BP
USA	UK

http://www.enslow.com

Library of Congress Cataloging-in-Publication Data

Pringle, Laurence P.
  Chemical and biological warfare : the cruelest weapons / Laurence
Pringle—rev. ed.
      p. cm. — (Issues in focus)
  Includes index.
  Summary: Examines the history and development of chemical and
biological weapons and discusses their proliferation, association with
terrorism, and efforts to control their use.
  ISBN 0-7660-1241-7
  1. Chemical warfare—Juvenile literature. 2. Biological warfare—
Juvenile literature. [1. Chemical warfare. 2. Biological warfare.]
  I. Title. II. Issues in focus (Hillside, N.J.)
  UG447 .P759   2000
  358´.34—dc21
                                        99-040269

Printed in the United States of America

10 9 8 7 6 5 4 3 2 1

To Our Readers:
All Internet addresses in this book were active and appropriate when we
went to press. Any comments or suggestions can be sent by e-mail to
comments@enslow.com or to the address on the back cover.

Illustration Credits: AP/Wide World Photos, pp. 10, 18; Bureau
of Land Management, p. 34; Dover Pictorial Archive Series, p. 16;
Dr. Joan Nowicki, Smithsonian Institution, p. 50; Enslow
Publishers, Inc., p. 38; Harriet Goitein, p. 61; National Archives,
pp. 8, 21, 27, 40; PAHO/WHO, p. 33; United Nations, pp. 55,
64, 66, 67, 88, 90, 91; U.S. Army, p. 93; U.S. Department of
Agriculture, p. 74; U.S. Department of Defense, p. 58.

Cover Illustration: AP/Wide World Photos. This November
1990 photo shows soldiers from the 24th Mechanized Infantry
Brigade from Fort Stewart, Georgia, carrying their weapons as
they undergo chemical warfare training in eastern Saudi Arabia
during Operation Desert Shield.

Contents

Acknowledgment

The author thanks Roger Beaumont, professor of history at Texas A & M University, for reading the manuscript and helping to improve its accuracy.

Introduction to the Revised Edition

When *Chemical and Biological Warfare: The Cruelest Weapons* was published in 1993, it ended on a hopeful note. The Cold War was over, and the United States and nations of the former Soviet Union began destroying their chemical and biological weapons. Watched by United Nations' inspectors, Iraq seemed to have grudgingly stopped producing such arms. And many nations agreed to ban the production, acquisition, stockpiling, and use of chemical weapons.

As a new century begins, there is still reason for hope, but also cause for increased concern. Iraq still has production facilities for chemical and biological arms—and may have no intention of honoring the treaty barring their use. Also, the threat of bioterrorism is growing. In the 1990s a Japanese cult tried to kill millions of people by releasing disease germs and nerve gas in Tokyo. It failed, but the threat of germ warfare by small groups of people has caused growing concern. In the late 1990s the United States began training emergency teams in one hundred twenty cities to prepare for a terrorist attack using chemical or biological weapons.

This threat is explored in detail in an expanded and revised Chapter 6. New findings and developments are added throughout the book and especially to the later chapters of this revised edition.

Poison gases were a major, widely used weapon just once in history, during World War I.

1

"Mysterious,
Devilish Thing"

In the 1935–1936 war between Italy and Ethiopia, the Ethiopians feared artillery shells and bombs from aircraft, but were familiar with them. Then the Italian air force began dropping drums and bombs of poisonous gas and spraying a deadly rain of chemicals from low-flying airplanes. Ethiopia was defeated, partly because these chemical arms caused low morale among civilians and soldiers. A British observer wrote that poison gas was something outside the Ethiopians' experience, "a mysterious, devilish thing."

Both chemical and biological weapons can be called mysterious, devilish things.

Although exploding bombs, missiles, and artillery shells have caused much more death and destruction, clouds of toxic chemicals and the invisible deadliness of germ warfare frighten people almost as much as the ultimate horror: nuclear war.

Nuclear, chemical, and biological weapons have some similar qualities that frighten people. They are unfamiliar hazards that seem capable of killing or injuring many people at once. They also seem uncontrollable. Biological and some chemical weapons are invisible, as is nuclear radiation. These characteristics, and the fact that chemical and biological weapons are almost always used against defenseless populations, cause people to dread them.

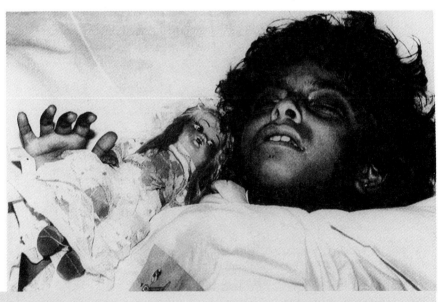

This Kurdish girl was one of many people injured in 1988 when Iraq used chemical weapons on its own people. She was a victim of mustard gas poisoning.

According to a 1969 United Nations report, chemical weapons are "chemical substances, whether gaseous, liquid, or solid, which might be employed because of their direct toxic effects on man, animals, and plants." Biological weapons are "living organisms, whatever their nature, or infective material derived from them, which are intended to cause disease or death in man, animals, or plants, and which depend for their effects on their ability to multiply in the person, animal, or plant attacked."

Since 1925, more than one hundred forty nations have signed an agreement called the Geneva Protocol barring the first use of chemical and biological weapons in war. Several nations have since ignored this accord because there is no provision for punishing nations who do so. During the early 1980s, for example, Iraq released poisonous gases against Iranian troops. Again in 1988 Iraq used chemical weapons to put down a rebellion of its own Kurdish citizens.

One outcome of the 1991 Persian Gulf War was that Iraq agreed to give up all materials and equipment for making chemical and biological weapons—but then broke the agreement. Furthermore, according to the United States Central Intelligence Agency (CIA), about twenty-five other nations have a chemical industry that enables them to make such weapons. In fact, some countries already have stockpiles of such arms.

The United States and other nations that have huge arsenals of conventional arms as well as nuclear weapons have urged these countries to destroy their chemical weapons' supply. To countries lacking conventional and nuclear arms, however, chemical and biological weapons have a special appeal. In the Middle East, for example, several Arab nations believe that they must have the option to make chemical weapons to counter the chemical and nuclear arms of Israel. Chemical and biological weapons are seen as an equalizer. They have been called "the poor man's atomic bomb" since they are cheaper and easier to produce than nuclear weapons.

Nasty as they are, chemical and biological weapons pose a limited threat in warfare—or have so far. But genetic engineering may enable scientists to create more deadly varieties of diseases from living organisms. These weapons could be more dangerous and crueler than those already in existence. Even without genetic changes, germ weapons pose a threat, from nations and from terrorist groups.

This book explores all of these matters and concludes with the great challenge facing earth's community of nations: to halt the production of chemical and biological weapons and to keep them from becoming an even greater menace.

2

From Smoke Screens to Mustard Gas

When were chemical or biological weapons first used in war? The answer may be before recorded history. Perhaps the first chemical weapon was smoke. Armies burned freshly cut wood and leaves in order to create smoke to conceal their advance, to force their opponents out of hiding, or even to suffocate their enemies in cave hideouts.

Beginning at least three thousand years ago, soldiers added chemicals to fires in order to produce fumes that choked or sickened enemies. Weapons based on fire were used in the Peloponnesian War, a conflict between different states in Greece

13

that began in 432 B.C. Armies laid siege to walled cities. A primitive flamethrower—fire propelled by bellows through a giant pipe—burned the wooden walls of one town. Defenders of the Greek city Syracuse made a highly flammable mixture of pitch, sulfur, pine sawdust, and other ingredients to destroy the Athenian battering rams that attacked their walls.

"Greek fire" was a chemical weapon, perhaps invented in A.D. 660 by a Greek engineer named Callinicus. It helped Byzantine Greeks repulse several attacks on the port city of Constantinople by Arabs and Russians. In A.D. 673, for example, a Saracen (Arab) fleet was nearly destroyed by jets of liquid fire emitted from tubes that protruded from Greek galleys. Water tossed on the flames only caused the fire to burn more fiercely.

The original "recipe" of Greek fire is not known. It probably included pitch, sulfur, quicklime, and *naphtha*—the Greek term for the petroleum that they collected from surface pools.

The First Biological Weapons

Biological warfare—using disease as a weapon—developed more recently than chemical warfare. Scientists did not prove that germs (bacteria, viruses, and rickettsia) cause infectious diseases until the nineteenth century. Long before then, however, people observed that some diseases seemed to be spread by contact with a sick or dead person or by drinking water contaminated with the decaying body of an animal. That knowledge was put to use in warfare; for example, enemies would throw human corpses or animal carcasses down wells to poison a population's water supply.

An early instance of biological warfare that was recorded in detail occurred in A.D. 1346. Tartars had laid siege to the port city of Caffa (now Feodosiya in the Ukraine) on the east coast of the Black Sea. Caffa was inhabited mostly by Italian merchants and soldiers, who showed no signs of weakening. Then a deadly infectious disease, the plague, struck the Tartars; thousands died. According to Italian historian Gabriel de Mussis, the Tartars turned their disease victims into weapons:

> The Tartars, fatigued by such a plague and pestiferous disease, stupefied and amazed, observing themselves dying without hope of health, ordered cadavers placed on their hurling machine and thrown into the city of Caffa, so that by means of these intolerable passengers the defenders died widely. Thus there were projected mountains of dead, nor could the Christians hide or flee, or be freed from such disaster. . . . And soon all the air was infected and the water poisoned, corrupt and putrified.

The Italians gave up the city. Then, fleeing to Italy by sea, the survivors unwittingly helped spread the deadly plague to Europe.

Biological warfare also helped European invaders defeat the natives of North America. During the French and Indian War, the commander in chief of the British forces urged that smallpox be spread to

Fiery chemical weapons were developed to defend and to attack walled cities and castles. But this knight on a horse was using the traditional weapon of the time to defend his city.

the Indians. "You will do well to try to inoculate the Indians by means of blankets," he wrote to the commander of Fort Pitt, which was located where the city of Pittsburgh, Pennsylvania, now stands. In 1763 a British captain met with two Indian chiefs and gave them gifts of blankets that had been brought from a smallpox hospital. According to historians, smallpox soon raged among the tribes of the region.

Overall, however, chemical weapons have been further developed and more frequently used than biological weapons. The British fired artillery shells loaded with picric acid during the Boer War (1899–1902) in southern Africa. The resulting fumes were not, however, an effective weapon.

Chlorine gas was proposed as a weapon for the Union forces during the Civil War in the United States. But Edwin Stanton, secretary of war, rejected a plan to fire chlorine-filled shells at Confederate troops. Some fifty years later, however, chlorine was used in modern warfare—with horrifying results that turned world opinion against chemical weapons.

Full Scale Gas Attacks

In 1915 World War I was at a stalemate, with opposing forces dug into trenches. Both sides had fired tear gas shells in unsuccessful efforts to dislodge their opponents. Near the Belgian city of Ypres, German forces were faced by French and Algerian troops. In the late afternoon of April 22, the wind was blowing toward the Allied trenches. German troops released 168 tons of liquid chlorine from nearly six thousand cylinders that they had hauled to the front lines under cover of darkness.

A yellow cloud of poisonous gas drifted across no-man's-land to the Allied lines. Heavier than air, the chlorine gas settled into the trenches and deep shelters where the Allied troops thought they were safe.

Chlorine gas irritates the eyes, nose, and throat. It blinded some soldiers and caused many others to choke to death. Still other soldiers ran in panic trying to escape the gas attack. They deeply inhaled the chlorine and also died, however. The attack killed

Canadian troops charge from a trench in World War I. In order to break the stalemate of trench warfare, Germany launched poison gas attacks.

an estimated five thousand men and wounded another ten thousand. It opened a four-mile-wide breach in the Allied front lines. The Germans had not expected such success, however, and did not have enough troops poised to exploit this opportunity.

Two days later German troops released more chlorine gas. This time the victims were Canadian troops, who had been given cloth, to be dipped in urine or bicarbonate of soda, for use as a primitive gas mask. Many died, but the Canadian forces were able to fend off attacking German troops. From April 1915 until the war's end in 1918, both sides rushed to develop and use poison gases and the defenses against them.

In late September 1915, British troops launched a chlorine gas attack on German positions in Belgium. It was a success, leading to the capture of more than three thousand German soldiers. However, it also illustrated a limitation and danger of chemical warfare that still affects military thinking. The wind had shifted and carried chlorine toward the British lines, causing casualties and an abrupt end to the gas attack. Over a three-week period, some twenty-four hundred British men were injured by the poison gas released by their own troops.

Poison gas attacks became a basic part of the war. Both sides fired artillery and mortar shells loaded with deadly chemicals. World War I became a chemical warfare test, with as many as fifty different types of gas used on the experimental animals—human beings. By late 1915 the Germans were using phosgene, an almost invisible gas that causes victims to choke, gasp for air, and suffocate. That form of gas smells like new-mown hay but is ten times as deadly as chlorine. Within months the British were also launching phosgene attacks.

Troops on both sides, and even cavalry horses and mules, now wore improved gas masks. Gas attacks, consequently, became less effective. Sometimes, to overcome this defense, two gases were released together. The Germans mixed chloropicrin, which penetrated masks well, with phosgene. Chloropicrin caused nausea and vomiting. When the soldiers raised their gas masks to throw up, they would inhale the deadly phosgene.

In July 1917, Germany took the lead in the chemical arms race. German soldiers attacked—again near Ypres, Belgium—with a new gas delivered in artillery shells. The new and more deadly weapon was dichloroethyl sulfide, known simply as mustard gas or just mustard. In concentrated form it has the sharp smell of mustard or horseradish.

Bursting shells spewed out an oily brown liquid and an acrid gas. At first the substances seemed harmless. Many Allied soldiers removed their masks. Within a few hours, however, mustard gas began to cause vomiting, severe burns, and temporary blindness. Gas masks were effective at preventing internal injuries, but the gas could seep into boots and penetrate several layers of cloth, causing huge blisters.

Within three weeks, German mustard gas attacks had caused fifteen thousand British casualties. Mustard became known as the "king of the war gases," partly because it persisted in liquid form for days after being released. The Germans used it for defensive purposes, in an attempt to create mustard-splattered zones to block the forward movement of Allied forces.

Near the war's end, Allied forces were also attacking with mustard gas. One casualty was a young courier named Adolf Hitler, who later wrote, in *Mein Kampf*, of his experience of being temporarily blinded. By 1918 artillery barrages often included as many gas shells as high-explosive shells. Altogether, 113,000 tons of poison gases were used in World War I. Chemical warfare caused an estimated 92,000 deaths and 1.3 million total

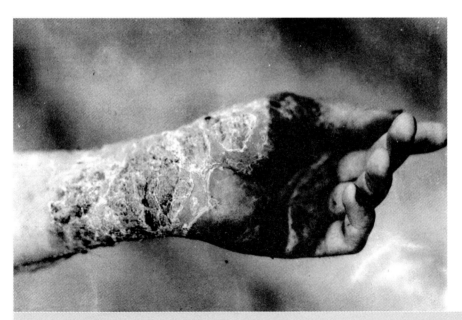

As gas masks became more effective, the warring nations tried new types of gases, including mustard, which causes the wound shown.

casualties. Some mustard gas residue lasted for a decade. Total casualties during World War I were 21 million but, military historians agree, chemical arms did not have a decisive effect on the outcome of the war.

The First Attempt to Ban Chemical Weapons

The use of chemicals did, however, have other effects. One was global revulsion toward chemical warfare. The end of World War I marked the beginning of an effort in the League of Nations to outlaw chemical weapons. The result was the 1925 Geneva Protocol. (Its full name is "Protocol for the prohibition of the use in war of asphyxiating, poisonous, or other gases, and of bacteriological methods of warfare.") Some one hundred forty nations (including Iraq) have signed this accord. Although it has discouraged the use of chemical weapons, it has several loopholes.

One loophole is that the protocol has no provision for punishing nations that use chemical or biological weapons. Another is that it does not prohibit making and storing such arms or threatening to use them. A third flaw is the protocol's vagueness about what it prohibits. Should "other gases" include tear gases, or the herbicides that the United States rained down on Vietnam? In 1969 eighty-nine countries in the United Nations voted in favor of including such "nonlethal" weapons, but their vote was only a recommendation, not binding on parties of the Geneva Protocol.

Many survivors of World War I poison gas attacks

lived with horrible memories of that moment when the toxic clouds billowed toward them or when mustard blistered their skin. Many suffered chronic illnesses, scarred lungs, or an early death. For these survivors, and for the dead, the first attempt to outlaw chemical and biological weapons came too late to help.

3

Nerve Gases and Germ Warfare

The United States first sent troops to Europe in June 1917, and seventy thousand soldiers were victims of gas attacks. At military facilities in Maryland, the United States began producing great quantities of its own chemical weapons. The war ended, however, before they were put to use.

Between 1935 and 1936, as mentioned, the Italian air force sprayed mustard gas from airplanes flying over Ethiopia. It also dropped bombs that exploded two hundred feet above the ground, releasing a mist of mustard on Ethiopian soldiers and civilians. Between

24

1937 and 1945, Japan, too, used poison gases against unprotected peasants and soldiers during its invasion and occupation of China. The Japanese also engaged in biological warfare. This was the first documented case of germ warfare since the British attempt to spread smallpox among American Indians 174 years earlier.

Japan's Germ Warfare

In the 1990s some details were finally revealed about Japan's use of biological weapons. Experiments on the effectiveness of germ weapons were carried out by Unit 731 of the Japanese Imperial Army. The research and testing sites were in Manchuria, a region of northeast China that Japan had conquered. Apparently the sites were chosen because they were far from Japan (posing no threat to Japanese people), and because they were near a plentiful supply of research subjects, mostly Chinese and Russian prisoners, with some Americans as well. These victims were called marutas—"logs." In 1999 a former officer of Unit 731, Toshimi Mizobuchi, said, "They were logs to me. Logs were not considered to be human. They were either spies or conspirators."

Japan's program was huge. It used one hundred fifty buildings and more than three thousand scientists and technicians. At least three thousand and perhaps as many as ten thousand people died in Japanese tests of biological and chemical weapons. Using knowledge from this research, Japan waged biological and chemical warfare against the Chinese people. Japan attacked hundreds of heavily populated communities with bombs containing plague-infected fleas or germs of anthrax, typhoid, or other diseases. They also dropped typhoid and cholera germs in wells. The death toll remains in dispute. Some scholars say that at least two hundred thousand Chinese died. Others believe the total was much lower.

The Japanese learned, as the British did with chlorine gas in 1915, that chemical and biological weapons can sometimes harm the forces that use them. This is called the boomerang effect. In 1942 nearly two thousand Japanese soldiers died in one Chinese province from diseases that had been deliberately spread by the Japanese.

Japan's biological and chemical attacks in China were the only use of such weapons in World War II. This fact is remarkable. Both sides battling for control of Europe had stockpiles of deadly chemicals. Clearly, the potential for all-out chemical war was there, but both sides feared retaliation.

New Weapons: Nerve Gases

Germany had developed new chemical arms that could have killed many thousands of Allied troops. German scientists had discovered that chemicals related to insecticides, called tabun, sarin, and soman, were also nerve gases. Tabun was the first nerve gas and one that Germany produced in great amounts during World War II. (The others, developed a few years later, were even more deadly.)

Colorless and odorless, nerve gases can be

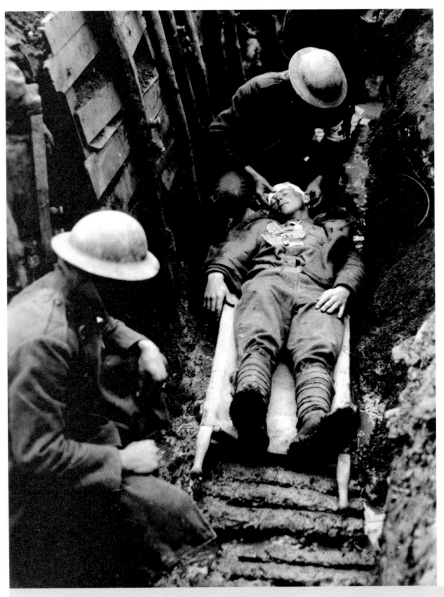

Chemical weapons caused one quarter of all United States casualties in World War I.

inhaled or absorbed through the skin. Within the body, they block the action of an enzyme that serves to end transmission of nerve impulses. The result is wild, uncontrollable nerve signals to muscles, including those that control breathing. Victims lose control of their bodies. Violent convulsions are soon followed by suffocation.

Nazi Germany had more than twelve thousand tons of one such gas stockpiled by 1945. Historians have speculated about why none of these horrible weapons was used. Perhaps the reason was that Germany's military commanders believed that the United States and other Allied powers had nerve gases, too, and feared retaliation. Also, late in the war when Germany might have taken desperate steps to turn the tide of battle, its air force was too weak to deliver a major nerve gas attack.

Germany's information about the Allies having nerve gases was wrong. Both the United States and Great Britain did, however, have great quantities of mustard and other chemical weapons. In 1944 the prime minister of Great Britain, Winston Churchill, urged his commanders to study the possibility of "drenching" German cities with toxic gases. This chemical warfare was never carried out; nor did Great Britain use the biological weapons it had begun to produce in the late 1930s.

Biological Weapons in the United States

In the United States, research on biological weapons began in 1942 at a Maryland army camp, now called

Fort Detrick. Scientists began studying ways to make weapons of diseases such as typhus, cholera, yellow fever, plague, anthrax, and botulism. The last two initially received the most attention. Both anthrax and botulism originate with bacteria, strike quickly, and can be deadly.

Aided by the British, the United States developed the first biological bomb in 1943. It weighed four pounds and contained anthrax spores. Soon United States scientists had also made bombs containing botulism toxin, a deadly poison that people sometimes consume in food. Had the United States chosen to do so, it had the capacity to make many thousands of anthrax or botulism bombs each month.

Near the end of the war in Europe, United States scientists were also trying to make a weapon of brucellosis, or undulant fever. Caused by a bacterium, undulant fever is seldom fatal but can make people ill for months. The United States also had developed several chemicals for use against plants, specifically, against rice crops in Japan.

Plans for destroying Japan's rice crop from the air were still under study in the summer of 1945. They were never put into action. Instead, another kind of new weapon, the atomic bomb, was dropped on two Japanese cities. Japan surrendered in mid-August 1945.

The Cold War Begins

Soon after the end of World War II, the United States was engaged in another, different kind of war—the so-called Cold War of hostile, suspicious relations between the Western powers and the communist-run Soviet Union and its allies. The Soviets had captured a nerve gas factory in eastern Germany, disassembled it, and had it reassembled in Russia. In Japan, the United States also scored a coup: It captured the leaders of Japan's biological warfare program.

In 1949 the Soviet Union accused the United States of protecting the leaders of Japan's inhumane germ warfare research on American and other prisoners of war. The United States dismissed the charge as propaganda. But documents released in later years show that the accusation was accurate; a deal had been made. Japanese researchers, even though they had probably committed war crimes, were not prosecuted. In return the United States obtained details of the only known research on the effects of biological weapons on human subjects. By avoiding a war crimes trial, the United States was able to keep this information secret.

Fear of communism fueled United States research on chemical and biological weapons. In 1960 the head of United States Army research claimed that a massive effort to produce chemical arms was under way in the Soviet Union. The United States budget for research and development of such weapons soared. It grew from about $10 million a year in the early 1950s to $352 million in 1969. Many of these funds were spent on tear gas and herbicides used in the Vietnam War. Chinese Communists and Koreans claim the United States used germ warfare during the Korean War. Some researchers worked for the military at Fort Detrick and other facilities; others worked for some three hundred private companies, research institutes, and universities.

A variety of chemical and biological weapons were developed. They included nerve gases that could be released from land mines, and saxitoxin, a deadly shellfish poison, placed on the tips of scores of bullet-size darts that exploded in all directions from a five-hundred-pound cluster bomb. At Fort Detrick scientists learned how to raise five hundred thousand *Aedes aegypti* mosquitoes a month and infect them with yellow fever. They planned, but never built, a plant that each month could have developed 130 million of these disease-carrying mosquitoes.

Testing Bioweapons on United States Citizens

Most of the research on biological weapons was a well-kept secret until the 1970s, when many government documents were released as a result of the Freedom of Information Act. It was not until 1977 or later that the public learned that many people had served as guinea pigs, beginning in 1951. These tests are described in detail in Leonard Cole's *Clouds of Secrecy: The Army's Germ Warfare Tests Over Populated Areas*.

To learn how to detect biological warfare agents, and also to find the most effective ways to spread them among a population, the United States military decided to conduct secret open-air tests using live microorganisms. Some of this research was conducted far from population centers; for example, at the Dugway Proving Ground in Utah. Some research was conducted in major United States cities.

In 1955 the CIA obtained supplies of whooping cough bacteria from Fort Detrick, and then conducted studies along the Gulf Coast of Florida. According to Florida's medical records, the number of cases of whooping cough tripled that year. There were 339 cases and one death in 1954; 1,080 cases and twelve deaths in 1955. The CIA also conducted tests of mind-altering drugs such as LSD on hundreds of people without their knowledge.

As a rule, however, military researchers used what they called biological simulants in their tests on unsuspecting people. These were bacteria or other microorganisms that behaved like disease-causing organisms, but which were believed to be harmless. For example, to simulate a biological warfare attack in the United States, scientists used bacteria called *Bacillus subtilis*. It has many of the characteristics of *Bacillus anthracis*, which causes anthrax. Defending the use of this simulant in 1977, army researchers said that there was no evidence that it was harmful to people. Nevertheless, there were warnings in the medical reference books that *subtilis* sometimes caused infections.

This sort of research went on for two decades, from 1949 to 1969. Millions of people were exposed to several varieties of bacteria released in more than two hundred thirty populated areas. The test sites included Minneapolis, St. Louis, Washington, D.C.,

The Aedes aegypti *mosquito carries yellow fever and could be bred in huge numbers to be released as a biological weapon.*

and the New York City subway system. Army researchers made no attempt to monitor the health of target populations. When the secret tests were finally revealed, during United States Senate hearings in 1977, army spokesmen continued to argue that these bacteria were harmless. Doctors who testified disagreed. They said that exposure to heavy concentrations of even supposedly harmless bacteria can cause illness and that the secret tests had been a health hazard.

An incident in 1968 drew the attention of news media and the public to the United States biological and chemical weapons research. VX nerve gas was being released from a jet aircraft flying low over a target area at Dugway Proving Ground, Utah. As the

An accidental release of nerve gas killed herds of sheep in Utah. This 1968 incident drew attention to United States research on chemical and biological weapons.

jet climbed to a higher altitude, about twenty pounds of the nerve gas was accidentally dispersed. Winds carried the VX gas eastward more than thirty-five miles to an area where sheep grazed. Six thousand sheep died or had to be slaughtered because of possible contamination.

The government denied responsibility for several months, which only intensified questioning from news media and the public. Finally, army researchers admitted the accident. The victims were sheep, not people, but this mistaken release of nerve gas fueled opposition to research on chemical and biological weapons.

4

Agent Orange and Yellow Rain

In the late 1960s the United States had a large arsenal of chemical and biological weapons, but opposition to the program grew in Congress. The Vietnam War was an underlying cause for this change. As the war dragged on, more and more people questioned the tactics of the United States' forces and even their presence in Southeast Asia. America's use of chemical weapons helped erode public confidence in the United States' involvement.

The weapons were types of tear gas and herbicides (plant-killing chemicals). The United States contended that these chemicals were not the sort prohibited by the Geneva Protocol. However, the ways in which massive amounts of these compounds were used led many scientists and other people to oppose this kind of warfare.

Use of Tear Gases in Vietnam

Use of chemical weapons began on a small scale in 1962, when the United States supplied the South Vietnamese Army with riot control gases (sometimes called tear gases, irritant agents, or harassing agents). The most common was called CS. By 1965 United States troops were using CS to force enemy soldiers from their networks of underground tunnels and bunkers. In a confined space, CS and other tear gases do not easily disperse and can be as lethal as other chemical weapons.

Eventually CS was also used for defensive purposes; for example, in booby traps around the perimeter of a camp. As an offensive weapon, CS was released in fifty-five-gallon drums from helicopters. Just before a B-52 bomb attack or a sweep by ground forces, vast amounts of CS were dispersed over forested areas, in hopes of driving the Communist Vietcong forces out into the open.

Agent Orange and Other Plant Killers

Some 13.7 million pounds of CS were used in the Vietnam War. Between 1962 and 1971 the United States also drenched Vietnam and parts of neighboring Laos with nearly 19 million gallons of herbicides. They were called Agents Blue, White, Purple, and

Orange. Agents Purple and Orange were a mixture of two plant-killing chemicals that in 1970 were banned in the United States because they were judged to be hazardous to human health.

President John F. Kennedy had approved the use of these herbicides in late November 1961. The chemical-spraying program, called Operation Ranch Hand, was aimed at destroying crops to deny the enemy food and to defoliate trees to deny the enemy cover. Agent Blue killed rice plants, and Agent White slowly killed trees. Agents Purple and Orange quickly killed the leaves of trees and shrubs.

Between 1962 and 1971 Operation Ranch Hand sprayed nearly 6 million acres of South Vietnam. Almost 90 percent of the herbicides were used to defoliate forests. Wide swaths were sprayed alongside roads and railroads in an attempt to reduce the threat of ambushes. Herbicides also rained down around base camps to aid their defense and on forests where enemy camps or infiltration routes were hidden.

Questions About Herbicides

Although the United States military continued to support this program, some military experts questioned its value. Defoliation may have actually improved the field of fire for ambushers and removed cover in which ambushed troops could hide. The sharpest criticism, however, was aimed at crop spraying.

Interviews with civilians and former Vietcong

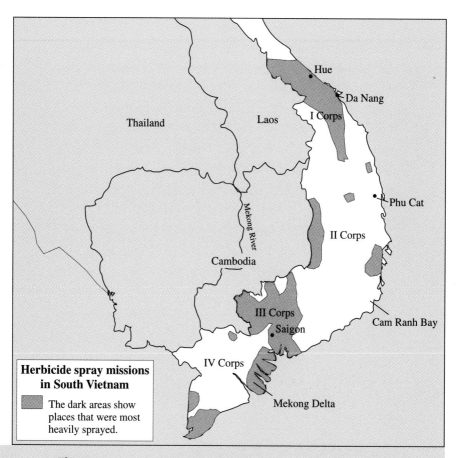

Herbicide spray missions in South Vietnam

The dark areas show places that were most heavily sprayed.

This map is a representation of herbicide spray missions during the Vietnam War. The dark areas represent concentrated spraying areas. This map only represents fixed-wing aircraft spraying, and does not include helicopter spraying of perimeters, or other spray methods. The III Corps area received the heaviest concentrations of spraying, followed by I Corps, II Corps, and IV Corps.

soldiers showed that crop spraying did not cause any serious food shortages for enemy troops. The crop destruction did, however, cause hardship for many peasants and their families. It also increased their bitter feelings toward the United States and the South Vietnam government.

By the mid-1960s, scientists were increasingly concerned about herbicide use in Vietnam. They first worried about the long-term effects on forests and cropland, and later about the effects of dioxin—a highly toxic substance present in Agent Orange—on the health of civilians. Eventually, thousands of United States Vietnam veterans claimed that their health had been impaired by exposure to Agent Orange.

The damage included a higher risk of fathering children with spina bifida, a serious spinal birth defect. The dioxin in Agent Orange has also been associated with three types of cancer: soft-tissue sarcoma, non-Hodgkin's lymphoma, and Hodgkin's disease. A report by the United States Institute of Medicine also indicated a possible link with some skin diseases; PCT, a liver disorder; respiratory cancer; prostate cancer; and multiple myeloma. None of these claims, however, has ever been proven.

In early 1967 more than five thousand United States scientists signed a petition that urged an end to the use of CS and plant-killing chemicals in Vietnam. Their views joined countless others' from home and abroad. In 1969 the United Nations passed a resolution stating that the Geneva Protocol prohibited "any chemical agents of warfare . . . which might be employed because of their direct

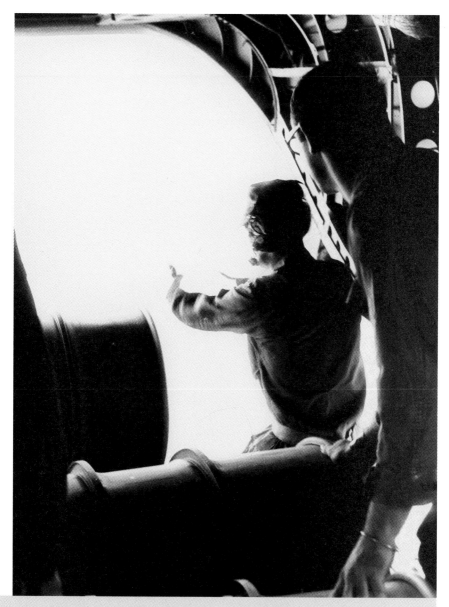

*The tear gas CS was used as an offensive weapon in the
Vietnam War. Here, barrels of CS are dropped from a helicopter.*

toxic effects on humans, animals, or plants." This was clearly aimed at the United States' use of herbicides. Eighty-nine nations voted for this resolution. Only the United States and two other countries voted against it, although thirty-six nations—mostly United States allies—abstained from voting.

Members of Congress threatened major cuts in funds for chemical and biological weapons. President Richard Nixon ordered a review of the United States program, and in November 1969 he announced major changes. The United States would stop making biological weapons and destroy its stocks of them. It would, however, continue to study defenses against such weapons. The United States would also give up first use of chemical arms, using them only in response to a chemical attack. Many nations that have ratified the Geneva Protocol take this position also.

The United States continued to claim that herbicides and CS gases were not lethal weapons, and would still be used in Vietnam. Their use was phased out, however.

Worry About Biological Weapons

Public outrage and protests from scientists were not the only reasons for the dramatic change in United States policy. Another reason was the realization that development of biological weapons might, in the long run, harm United States interests. Biological weapons can be produced cheaply. According to a report to the United Nations in 1969 (using 1969 prices), in a large-scale military attack on civilians, "casualties might cost about $2,000 per square kilometer with conventional weapons, $800 with nuclear weapons, $600 with nerve gas weapons, and $1 with biological weapons."

Poor nations with biological arms could easily gain highly destructive weapons. This would change the world's balance of power. Matthew Meselson, an expert on such weapons and a professor of biochemistry at Harvard University, wrote in 1964, "The introduction of radically cheap weapons of mass destruction into the arsenals of the world would not act as much to strengthen the big powers as it would endow dozens of relatively weak countries with great destructive capacity."

The Biological Weapons Treaty

Thus the United States had a strong incentive to discourage the spread of biological and chemical arms. It showed renewed interest in negotiating a new international agreement on this matter. The treaty, completed in 1971 and proposed for ratification in 1972, is called the Biological and Toxin Weapons Convention. The Biological and Toxin Weapons Convention, which took effect in 1975, was a major step in disarmament. It prohibits development, production, and stockpiling of biological arms as well as their use. This includes toxins, which are poisonous substances produced by bacteria and other living organisms.

More than one hundred fifty nations have agreed

to its terms. The Biological and Toxin Weapons Convention is stronger than the Geneva Protocol, but it, too, has troublesome loopholes. It lacks procedures for verifying complaints that a nation is breaking its rules. And the defensive research it allows—for example, developing vaccines and protective gear against germ warfare diseases—can have offensive uses as well.

In its introduction, the Biological and Toxin Weapons Convention asserted that it was a first possible step toward a similar treaty prohibiting the development and stockpiling of chemical arms. The United States and the Soviet Union began to negotiate the terms of this treaty, which became the Chemical Weapons Convention of 1993.

In 1972 the Chemical Corps of the U.S. Department of Defense was closed. Its stocks of biological weapons were destroyed and its production plants shut down. The Department of Defense budget for chemical and biological arms shrank to about $75 million, a modern low, in 1975.

The Department of Defense, and supporters of the Chemical Corps in Congress, began to emphasize a new way to deliver deadly chemicals called binary munitions. Actually, United States research on these weapons has been traced to 1949. Binary weapons consist of two chemical compounds that mix and produce a nerve gas within an artillery shell or other munitions while it is in flight. For battlefield troops, it was claimed, these weapons would be safer to use than other chemical arms. They would also be safer to store and transport, whether in battle or in peacetime near civilian populations.

Financial support for chemical warfare research began to rise dramatically in 1980, the year Ronald Reagan was elected president. Cold War tensions had grown in the late 1970s, and President Reagan held rigid anti-Soviet views. There was increased worry—or paranoia—that the Soviets were disregarding the Biological and Toxin Weapons Convention and forging ahead with new and more deadly chemical and biological weapons.

First Reports of Yellow Rain Attacks

Beginning in 1978, newspaper reports from Thailand told of Laotian refugees who claimed that their villages had been attacked with poison gases from communist aircraft. The U.S. Department of State sent officers to interview some of the refugees, who said that the gases from exploding bombs or rockets, or those sprayed from planes, caused vomiting, diarrhea, and sometimes death. Other symptoms were also reported. A United States Army medical team also interviewed some refugees. Its report was made public in December 1979. It concluded that two or three chemical weapons had been used, including a nerve gas. The report also claimed that perhaps as many as one thousand Laotian refugees had died.

Rebels in Afghanistan also reported that Soviet troops had used chemical weapons. These reports, and those from Southeast Asia, fueled the Reagan administration's belief that the Soviets could not be trusted to honor treaties. In September 1981, then secretary of state Alexander Haig claimed that the United States had physical evidence that the Soviet Union and its allies had used highly toxic poisons in Southeast Asia.

The U.S. Department of State soon revealed its evidence. In addition to the interviews with refugees, there was a leaf and a stem collected from Cambodia covered with tiny yellow dots. The alleged poison came to be called "yellow rain." Analysis of these yellow spots on the leaf and stem was reported to show the presence of three lethal mycotoxins— poisons produced by fungi. Furthermore, the United States claimed that these mycotoxins did not occur naturally in Southeast Asia.

A Department of State report in March 1982 declared, "The conclusion is inescapable that the toxins and other chemical warfare agents were developed in the Soviet Union." The Reagan administration and its supporters in Congress began to routinely refer to "Soviet use of chemicals in Southeast Asia." Opposition to chemical arms declined in Congress, and increased funds were voted on for their development.

Anthrax Disaster at Sverdlovsk

An incident in the Soviet Union, first reported in late 1979, also added to suspicions that the Soviets were violating the Biological and Toxin Weapons Convention. In the city of Sverdlovsk (now called Yekaterinburg, its original name), there were reports that hundreds of people had died from anthrax. The Soviet government said that the anthrax outbreak was caused by contaminated meat. The Reagan administration claimed that the anthrax spores had escaped after an accidental explosion at a secret biological warfare plant.

Some scientists were skeptical about the evidence used to support the charge of Soviet treaty violations. The epidemic could have arisen from natural causes; anthrax was a public health problem in the Soviet Union, and there had been past outbreaks in the Sverdlovsk region. Only in 1992, after the Soviet Union broke up, was the truth known. President Boris Yeltsin of Russia admitted that the anthrax breakout had been the result of an accident at a germ warfare plant.

Further details became known in 1994 when a team of United States and Russian scientists studied hospital records and other evidence at Yekaterinburg. A tiny amount of anthrax spores had escaped from a Soviet biological weapons plant and had been carried by winds in a southeasterly direction. Within a few weeks at least sixty-six people died of anthrax, while others recovered. Numerous sheep and cattle also died.

Doubts About Yellow Rain

The United States' case against the Soviets in Southeast Asia, however, eventually unraveled. Some journalists and scientists questioned the scant evidence. For example, the Department of State based its case partly on a claim that yellow rain mycotoxins did not occur naturally in Southeast Asia. But experts on fungi said that the source of the mycotoxins, a fungus called *Fusarium*, could be found almost everywhere, including tropical Asia.

Some military experts wondered why mycotoxins would be chosen for biological warfare. Whether the goal was to kill people, make them ill, or terrify them, other kinds of chemical weapons would have been more effective.

The main physical evidence was the yellow spots on one leaf and stem. Eventually, many more yellow rain samples were collected and analyzed by government laboratories in the United States and Great Britain. No mycotoxins were found. Government labs in France and Sweden had the same results. Could the initial test have been in error? This seemed more and more likely.

Nevertheless, the Reagan, and later the Bush, administration expressed no doubts about its evidence. In November 1982 the Department of State sent a report entitled "Chemical Warfare in Southeast Asia and Afghanistan: An Update" to Congress and the United Nations. At a news briefing about the report, a Department of State official confirmed what several scientists had found: Yellow rain samples contained pollen. This was not tiny windborne pollen, but larger grains of the sort that bees and other insects collect from flowers.

A government expert on poisons explained that the Soviets mixed mycotoxins, a solvent, and pollen. The solvent helped the toxins penetrate human skin.

It was, she said, a "very clever mixture." A Department of State spokesman also said, "I have no idea how the Soviets produce this stuff. We've not been in their factory."

Communist Weapon—Or Bee Droppings?

United States accusations that yellow rain was a communist weapon continued, but facts to the contrary kept popping up. Thomas Seeley, a biologist at Yale University who had studied bees in Southeast Asia, hearing a description of the yellow, pollen-filled spots on leaves, identified them as bee droppings.

In 1984 Thomas Seeley, Matthew Meselson (an early doubter of the government's case), and a Thai bee expert went into Thailand forests to learn more about yellow rain. They observed showers of honeybee feces that were mostly the outer shells of pollen grains. Bees digest the protein and fats within the pollen grain, then defecate the rest.

Bee experts came forward with more information about the mass "cleansing" flights of honeybees. In the tropics, according to a Canadian biologist, honeybees excrete waste as a way to cool their bodies. This helps keep the temperature within their colonies low enough so their larvae develop normally. Cleansing flights occur anywhere honeybees live, including Washington, D.C., where scientists found spots of yellow rain on cars parked near a honeybee colony. Chinese scientists had been aware of these harmless showers of bee feces since 1976. In fact,

Chinese people were the first to use the term *yellow rain*.

Yellow rain had been proven to be bee feces. Physical evidence of chemical attacks from both Southeast Asia and Afghanistan was of dubious value. What, then, accounted for the claims of deaths, illness, and other details of chemical attacks? That evidence proved to be unreliable, too.

Government documents showed that United States interviewers failed to conduct impartial surveys. Hearsay was mixed with personal accounts. Also, many of the Laotian refugees were former members of an army supported by the CIA. They knew in advance that the interviewers wanted to hear about chemical attacks. Refugees who were interviewed more carefully a second time said that they had not witnessed any chemical attacks or victims.

Nicolas Wade, a specialist in science affairs for *The New York Times*, wrote an editorial on August 30, 1985, titled, "Rains of Error."

"Yellow rain is bee excrement," he wrote, "a fact so preposterous and so embarrassing that even now the Administration cannot bring itself to accept it."

United States presidents have a wealth of scientific expertise at their disposal, including the National Academy of Sciences. In the case of yellow rain, however, the Reagan administration does not seem to have carried out a careful scientific investigation before claiming that the Soviet Union was conducting chemical warfare.

The Reagan administration's scare tactics had the desired effect. The administration's accusations

Pollen grains, shown magnified about six hundred times, make up the bulk of honeybee feces, and of the alleged poison that was called "yellow rain."

changed United States government policy on chemical warfare. In 1985 Congress authorized funds to produce binary chemical weapons. The first nerve gas artillery shells were produced in December 1987. The United States had ended its eighteen-year-long moratorium on producing chemical weapons. However, the weapons have not been put into use.

5

Lessons From the Middle East

An arms control treaty can be a fragile thing. The treaty's strength is diminished when a nation flouts its rules and uses forbidden weapons. It is further weakened if other countries then do little to censure or punish the treaty-breaker. A treaty's strength can also be diminished when one nation makes false claims against another, using the arms control agreement as a political tool.

The Geneva Protocol and the Biological and Toxin Weapons Convention were harmed by the Reagan administration's unproven yellow rain accusations against the Soviet Union. These arms

52

control agreements were also hurt when the United States and other world powers almost completely ignored outbreaks of chemical warfare in the Middle East.

The Middle East is home to about one third of all countries that are capable of producing chemical weapons or are suspected of having them. These nations are Iraq, Iran, Syria, Israel, Libya, Ethiopia, and Egypt. Iraq had chemical and biological arms in 1991, but was supposed to destroy them to comply with the cease-fire agreement of the Persian Gulf War—a process that was still not complete nine years later, at the turn of the century.

Egypt's Use of Chemical Weapons

The most recent uses of chemical arms have also occurred in the Middle East. In the fall of 1962 Egypt entered a civil war in Yemen, battling Royalist forces that wanted to restore their leader to power. The Royalists controlled the mountains and other rugged terrain. They fought well, the war dragged on, and Egypt decided mustard attacks might settle matters quickly. In 1963 aircraft dropped mustard on several villages. Mostly civilian targets were chosen, perhaps because Royalist troops usually hid in caves. A British advisor to the Royalists said that he had seen and photographed "hideous sores and eruptions on the skin of children and animals who had been exposed to the gas." Egypt denied that any gas attacks had occurred, and only a few more were reported until the fall of 1966. Then mustard attacks resumed and increased in the spring and summer of 1967. Bombs containing mustard, and perhaps another chemical agent, fell on many villages, killing or injuring thousands of civilians. The Royalists showed no sign of weakening, however, and Egypt withdrew its forces from Yemen.

Despite abundant evidence that Egypt had used chemical weapons, no country made a formal protest to the United Nations. In 1967 Egypt had been crushed by Israel in the Six-Day War. Rather than upset complex political alliances with Middle Eastern nations, governments chose to ignore Egypt's gas warfare.

The Iraq-Iran War

In September 1980 Iraq invaded Iran, and an eight-year war began. As early as November 1980 Iran claimed that Iraq had dropped chemical bombs. At first Iraq conquered some Iranian territory. Then the Iranian army began to recover land that had been lost and to capture Iraqi soil. So the Iraqis stepped up their chemical attacks. Iran formally complained to the United Nations in late 1983, and a U.N. fact-finding team was sent in 1984 to inspect a battlefield site where chemical weapons were reportedly used. The investigating team also visited Iranian hospitals and examined victims.

The U.N. scientists reported their findings in March 1984. They had found bomb fragments and unexploded bombs, and the chemicals within these bombs proved to be mustard and the nerve gas tabun. This was the first time in history that a nerve gas was used in war.

The United Nations condemned this use of chemical arms, as did the United States, but Iraq continued its poison gas attacks through early 1988. (Iran reportedly retaliated briefly in 1988.) Iraq was on the defensive, outnumbered, and faced with massive Iranian "human wave" attacks. Some mustard attacks seemed to be aimed at contaminating the battlefield, creating a temporary barrier that Iranian troops would not cross. Besides killing and wounding Iranian soldiers, Iraq's chemical weapons affected

Rockets loaded with nerve gas were discovered and destroyed in Iraq by United Nations inspectors.

the Iranian troops' morale. Reportedly the sight of clouds from harmless smoke bombs was enough to cause Iranian troops to retreat.

The Iran-Iraq war ended in August 1988. Iran claimed nearly fifty thousand casualties and several thousand deaths from poison gas attacks. Aside from being scolded, however, Iraq was not punished for its use of illegal arms. Many governments were concerned about the militant power of Islamic Iran. Some, including the United States, were officially neutral but wanted Iraq and its leader, Saddam Hussein, to remain strong. No economic sanctions were imposed on Iraq, although the United States and several other nations banned the export to Iraq and Iran of certain chemicals that can be used to make chemical weapons. This made it more difficult but not impossible for Iraq to replenish its stocks of chemical arms.

In March 1988 Iraq attacked its own citizens with mustard and nerve gas. A Kurdish rebellion was put down after mustard caused a reported five thousand deaths in the Iraqi town of Halabja. Earlier, in 1987, Libya reportedly used chemical arms in a war with its neighbor Chad. Neither Libya nor Iraq suffered any harm from breaking the moral barriers of international law. They showed other Third World nations that these laws could be defied without punishment.

By the time Iraq invaded Kuwait in 1990, it had rebuilt its supplies and had the largest and most sophisticated chemical weapons program in the Third World. It could deliver chemical weapons from aircraft, or release them with artillery fire and rockets. Iraq was also believed to have biological weapons. As the United States and other countries in a coalition of allies prepared for the Persian Gulf War in 1990–1991, the threat of both poison gases and germ warfare was a cause of concern.

Defenses Against Chemical and Biological Weapons

Troops were vaccinated against anthrax. Masks and protective clothing also shielded soldiers from biological and chemical arms. The gas masks had two kinds of filters. One removed particles, including dangerous microorganisms. The other, made of activated charcoal, adsorbed molecules of chemical gas. (In adsorption, molecules stick to the charcoal's surface, and are not taken in, as when water is absorbed by a sponge.)

Troops also wore jackets and pants of two layers, with charcoal foam in the inner layer to trap toxic gases. They wore rubber gloves and overboots as well. In addition, they carried a package of medicated towelettes in case their skin was exposed to mustard gas or other blistering agents. And they also were given injectors that would give them a quick antidote against nerve gas.

Each soldier carried adhesive-backed paper strips, which could be stuck on their protective suits and that turned red when touched by poisonous chemicals. Troop units also had air sampling devices and alarms to warn of chemical attack. In addition,

United States forces had sixty German-built Fox chemical detection vehicles. These lightly armored and fast-moving vehicles were laboratories on wheels. They were equipped with sensors and a computer for detecting chemical agents in the air. The Foxes were expected to roam front lines and warn ground forces away from areas contaminated by chemicals.

There was great concern about the ability of United States and other coalition troops to function if a chemical attack forced them to wear their cumbersome protective clothing and gear. Daytime temperatures can reach 49°C (120°F) in the Arabian desert. The United States Army had specially made air-conditioned tents prepared to help soldiers cope with this problem.

United States soldiers maintain a desert outpost, dressed in gear designed to protect them from chemical and biological weapons.

Coalition forces were well protected, but their commanders worried about the combat-effectiveness of troops facing chemical attack. Gas masks impair vision and gloves impair the dexterity of fingers. Simple tasks, like digging a foxhole, and complicated ones, like rearming a helicopter, would take longer on a chemical battlefield. According to United States Army studies, this "operational degradation" could range from 30 percent to 50 percent.

All of this concern and preparation proved to be unnecessary. Despite repeated threats by President Saddam Hussein, Iraq never unleashed its arsenal of chemical weapons.

Although Iraqi gas masks and antidotes were left behind by retreating troops, Iraqi prisoners said that most of their units had inadequate protection against chemical attack. Allied aircraft had also dropped leaflets warning Iraqi commanders they would be held responsible if they used chemical weapons. Wind patterns and heavy rains may also have discouraged use of these weapons. So, too, did the swift success of Allied forces.

The Scud missiles Iraq launched toward Israel and Saudi Arabia were among the most dramatic elements of the war. Television viewers all over the world saw images of Israeli citizens wearing gas masks and taking shelter in sealed rooms. However, the missiles contained conventional explosives, not poison gases. Why? One explanation was that Iraq had not developed the needed technology, including a fuse that would cause a missile to explode and release a gas cloud before striking the ground.

Saddam Hussein may have feared alienating his Palestinian supporters in Israel. Chiefly, he had reason to fear chemical retaliation from the United States and its allies, or from Israel itself.

The Gulf War Syndrome

Soon after combat ended in the Persian Gulf War, in February 1991, many thousands of troops began to complain about a variety of symptoms: headaches, chronic fatigue, aching joints and muscles, digestive problems, rashes, memory loss, and short attention spans. The symptoms were experienced by troops of the United States and also of several other nations that had seen action against Iraq, and continued long after the soldiers returned to their home nations. Eventually more than 110,000 of the 700,000 American troops sent to the area suffered from some of these symptoms.

The symptoms were called the Gulf War Syndrome, and many victims wondered whether the cause was exposure to Iraq's chemical weapon arsenal. For five years the U.S. Department of Defense blamed the illnesses on psychological stress or exposure to oil well fires. It denied that American troops had been exposed to any chemical weapons. The voices of the victims were heard, however, and investigations unearthed evidence to the contrary. In 1996 a special White House panel condemned the Department of Defense, saying that it had "conducted a superficial investigation of possible chemical warfare

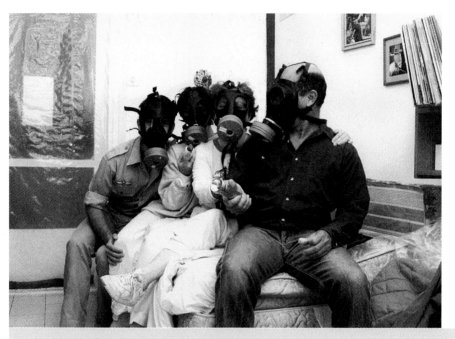

Warned of Scud missile attacks during the Persian Gulf War, Israelis donned gas masks and took shelter in sealed rooms.

exposures, which is unlikely to provide credible answers to veterans' questions."

The panel reported "overwhelming evidence that chemical weapons were released when American troops blew up a massive Iraq ammunition depot . . . in March 1991, shortly after the war. Thousands of American soldiers were deployed in the vicinity of the blast."

In 1996 it was estimated that twenty thousand troops had been exposed to chemical poisons from the demolition of the ammunition depot. This number was increased significantly in 1997, to an estimated ninety-eight thousand troops that had been in the plume of nerve gas from the arms depot. Further investigation revealed that American, French, and Czech units in charge of chemical detection had measured small amounts of sarin nerve gas and mustard gas in the air during the Gulf War. The poisons had not been deliberately released; they were detected soon after bombs fell on depots and factories where Iraq was known to store chemical and biological arms. In 1998 French scientists found traces of VX nerve gas on fragments of missiles that Iraq had partly destroyed in 1991.

The Department of Defense continued to claim there was no evidence that exposure to tiny amounts of sarin or other chemical weapons could cause Gulf War Syndrome. Its position, backed by some medical experts, was that strong doses of such weapons can cause death, though low doses are harmless. Other experts believed that small amounts of chemical weapons could be harmful, especially when victims were also exposed to other chemicals. In 1997, experiments with animals showed that exposure to a mixture of common chemicals in the air during the Gulf War could produce symptoms like those of the Gulf War Syndrome.

The chemicals were petroleum products (including smoke from oil well fires), pesticides (applied heavily by general spraying and by individual soldiers in the war), medical drugs and vaccines, and low doses of biological and chemical weapons. The very measures taken to protect troops from nerve gas may have caused health problems. An antinerve gas drug called pyridostigmine bromide given to all troops may have made their nervous systems more vulnerable to damage from a combination of chemicals.

Almost a decade after the war the mystery of the Gulf War Syndrome was still not solved, but it was the subject of many research projects. The discoveries that had been made raised questions about how best to protect troops in situations where they might be exposed to chemical and biological weapons.

Iraq Continues to Be a Threat

Soon after the war's end, Iraq reportedly used mustard against rebels among its own people, who tried to overthrow Saddam Hussein. A threat of United States air strikes stopped this tactic. Required by the United Nations to destroy its nuclear, chemical, and biological weapons, Iraq released its tally of chemical arms in April 1991. It admitted to having nearly ten thousand nerve gas warheads, more than one thousand tons of nerve and mustard gas, nearly fifteen hundred chemical bombs and shells, and thirty Scud missiles armed with chemical warheads.

Later in 1991, however, U.N. inspectors discovered that Iraq had many more chemical weapons than it had declared. This was just the first of many instances of Iraqi resistance to the terms of the U.N. cease-fire agreement. By 1995 the United Nations had learned that Iraq's germ warfare had been larger and more advanced than previously believed. During the 1991 war Iraq had bombs and Scud missiles armed with lethal germs, though it did

These Iraqi bombs, destroyed by the United Nations inspectors, had been equipped to carry chemical weapons.

not use them. It had plans for wiping out Israel's population with germ weapons and had tested various ways to disperse germs over Israel.

The U.N. inspection program was called UNSCOM, for United Nations Special Commission. Despite several years of noncooperation by Iraq, UNSCOM managed to find evidence that Iraq had hidden stores of chemical and biological weapons, and was probably still producing them. In 1998 Iraq became more defiant and devious about its chemical and biological weapons program. It forbade UNSCOM access to some sites, or delayed inspection until equipment could be moved and hidden. The crisis led to the withdrawal of inspectors, and bomb and missile attacks by the United States and Great Britain on suspected chemical and biological weapon sites. The threat of further destruction from the air remained, but without an UNSCOM program, Iraq was free to make biological and chemical arms in secret.

The Cruelest Weapons

Like World War II, the Persian Gulf War ended without the use of chemical weapons, even though both sides had such weapons. In the Middle East and elsewhere, there is a pattern in the history of chemical and biological warfare. Fear of retaliation, and knowing that one's enemy is well defended against chemical attack is a way to discourage a nation from using its chemical arms.

Throughout history, the victims of chemical and

Before UNSCOM ceased operations in 1998, its inspectors used cameras for twenty-four-hour monitoring.

UNSCOM made use of helicopters equipped with ground-penetrating radar in its investigation of Iraq's chemical and biological warfare program.

biological attacks have been troops or civilians who initially have no protection. Thus, chemical and biological arms may be the cruelest of all weapons.

This pattern will no doubt continue as long as chemical and biological arsenals exist. The most powerful nations will not need to use their stocks, but terrorists and Third World countries, acting aggressively or out of desperation, will be tempted to unleash their cruel weapons.

6

The Threat of Bioterrorism

The 1972 Biological and Toxin Weapons Convention was a remarkable achievement. It was the first arms control treaty calling for the destruction of an entire class of weapons. Furthermore, nations that signed it agreed never in any circumstances to develop, produce, stockpile, or otherwise acquire or retain microbes or other biological agents, or toxins, as well as weapons, equipment, or ways of delivering such agents or toxins for hostile purposes.

More than one hundred fifty nations have agreed to these terms, partly because biological weapons seem terrible and

69

inhumane, but also because military experts do not favor them. Germ weapons are dangerous to handle, difficult to spread effectively, and—once released—impossible to control.

This is as true today as it was in the early 1970s. However, interest in biological weapons has grown. The possibility of creating more deadly and manageable biological weapons now exists. So the United States, which has agreed to the terms of the Biological and Toxin Weapons Convention, now argues that it must study ways of detecting such weapons and defending people against them.

Can New Germ Weapons Be Created?

The possibility of creating new varieties of biological weapons arose in the early 1970s, when scientists discovered how to combine the genetic materials of two organisms. They "spliced" a gene from one organism into the genetic material (DNA) of another. This created a new life form with characteristics of both organisms. They also developed ways of mass-producing these new life forms.

This new technology—called biotechnology or genetic engineering—has already been used to cheaply mass-produce insulin and vaccines that were once in short supply. In agriculture, progress has been made in improving crop yields and plant resistance to pests. Genetic engineering has enormous potential for good.

It also has great potential for harm, though not as great as some journalists and politicians have claimed. In 1984, for example, a reporter for *The Wall Street Journal* claimed that "Soviet scientists were attempting to recombine the venom-producing genes from cobra snakes with ordinary viruses and bacteria: such an organism would infect the body and surreptitiously produce paralytic cobra neurotoxin." In other words, a person would get the effects of a deadly cobra bite from a simple microorganism.

Experts say that this imagined threat is far-fetched, given the present nature of genetic engineering. Its dangers are not likely to come from creating brand-new diseases, but from modifying existing ones so that it will be easier to wage germ warfare. For example, genetic engineering could alter a deadly, but rare, disease organism into one that could be cheaply mass-produced. This is just one way in which genetic engineering could produce weapons of war. Others include the following:

- improving the ability of microorganisms to survive after being sprayed from ships or aircraft, or released from bombs or missiles.
- toughening viruses or other germs so that they can overcome the natural resistance of people, and even of troops that have been vaccinated against the germs. (This would be achieved by altering the antigens on the outer surface of a virus, a change that would also make the disease agent harder to detect and identify.)
- increasing the deadliness of a disease, for example, by changing the anthrax bacterium so that it produces a stronger toxin.

- producing a new variety of a disease that is not affected by existing vaccines (In 1997 Russian scientists disclosed that they had used genetic engineering to make a type of anthrax that made Russia's anthrax vaccine useless.)
- speeding up the action of a disease organism, so that it causes illness within hours rather than days
- changing a common, relatively harmless bacterium into one that produces toxins
- applying some of these kinds of changes to microbes that harm livestock or crop plants, so that a nation's food supply and economy could be damaged

The Secret Soviet Germ Weapon Program

Research on genetic engineering may lead to these changes, but only with a great investment of money and time. In the United States that investment began in the early 1980s, when the Department of Defense began awarding contracts for biotechnology research. The Reagan administration promoted this change by claiming that the Soviet Union was engaged in illegal work on biological weapons. It was. After the Soviet Union broke up in the early 1990s, former Soviet scientists revealed many details about its germ warfare program. Soon after signing the Biological and Toxin Weapons Convention in 1972, the Soviet Union redoubled its germ research and production. Bombs and missiles were ready to spread hundreds of tons of smallpox, plague, and anthrax. If delivered effectively, these germ weapons could have wiped out entire nations. And even as the once mighty Soviet Union was coming apart, scientists were conducting tests on animals of the Marburg virus, a highly contagious germ that kills by attacking every organ and tissue in the body.

Defensive and Offensive Research

By the late 1980s well over $100 million was spent each year for research on genetic engineering by the U.S. Department of Defense. According to this department, very little of its research is secret and all of it is defensive—as required by the Biological and Toxin Weapons Convention. A number of scientists have observed, however, that the line between defensive and offensive research is unclear and easily crossed.

To develop defenses against biological weapons, studies have included methods of detecting disease agents as well as countermeasures, such as protective clothing and vaccines. They have also included basic research on potential disease agents and on ways in which an enemy might try to deliver them. All of these studies could yield practical information for waging biological war. (In World War II, Japan's secret germ-warfare research was officially described as work on vaccines and ways to purify water.)

Growing Concern About Terrorists

Even with the end of the Cold War and the breakup of the Soviet Union, American interest in biological weapons research has remained high. Concern grew

Biological weapons can harm people directly or indirectly, by damaging their food supplies or cash crops, such as sugarcane.

about the spread of such weapons to Third World nations and to terrorist groups.

Terrorists or guerrilla army units could use biological weapons to contaminate water supplies, kill crops and livestock, and cause local epidemics. There have already been charges that such weapons have been used covertly by enemy agents. In 1971, for example, Cuba claimed that agents of the CIA had released several diseases. One was African swine fever virus, which broke out in two far-apart sites. To halt the epidemic, one half million pigs were slaughtered. Cuba also blamed the CIA for outbreaks of dengue fever, which made 350,000 people ill, and for diseases that harmed tobacco and sugarcane crops.

Whether or not these charges were true, the CIA is better able to attack in this way than a terrorist or guerrilla group. Biological weapons are relatively cheap but require more expertise to produce than most chemical or conventional weapons, such as bombs. Terrorists can make sophisticated bombs, but are not likely to splice genes and create new disease microbes. Even without genetic engineering, however, terrorists could produce large amounts of diseases that have the potential of causing many deaths and great panic. Several incidents in the 1980s and 1990s drew attention to this threat.

A Cult's Plan to Take Over the World

In March 1995 an obscure Japanese cult (religious sect) made headlines around the world by releasing sarin nerve gas in the Tokyo subway, killing twelve people and injuring more than five thousand. Investigators discovered that the cult had conducted a nerve gas test the previous year. In June 1994, sarin had killed seven people and numerous dogs and birds in the city of Matsumoto, west of Tokyo. Furthermore, in the early 1990s the cult had tried repeatedly to kill millions of people with germ weapon attacks in and near Tokyo.

The cult was named Aum Shinrikyo, which means "supreme truth." In Japan it had many thousands of members, including several with advanced science degrees. Its goal was to wipe out most of the earth's population with chemical and biological weapons. Members of the cult believed that those faithful to Aum Shinrikyo would be superhumans and would survive and take over the planet.

Aum Shinrikyo first chose germs, not chemicals, as weapons of mass destruction. Beginning in 1990 its scientists obtained potentially deadly germs, produced large amounts, and released them in Tokyo and nearby sites. The cult first tried botulism and sprayed mists of this microbe from trucks, but no one died. There are many strains of botulism, and only a few have powerful toxins.

Anthrax was tried next. Pure anthrax can kill up to 90 percent of people who inhale its spores. A doctor in the cult obtained a sample of anthrax from a university. Huge amounts of anthrax were grown, then sprayed from trucks in Tokyo several times in 1993. Once again no one died. A relatively harmless strain of anthrax had been used, and sprayers clogged, failing to produce a fine mist of spores.

The final try with germ weapons refocused on botulism, which failed again. The cult also experimented with Q fever, and members traveled to Zaire in an attempt to get samples of the Ebola virus. This virus kills 70 percent of those it infects, advancing from a fever to massive blood hemorrhaging in ten days. After repeated failures with germ attacks—eight in all—the cult turned to sarin, and the 1995 gas attack led to arrests of cult leaders and revelations about Aum Shinrikyo's goals and actions.

Sources of Germ Weapons

Other incidents caused worry that groups, not nations, might use germ or chemical weapons to achieve their goals. In 1984 a religious cult in Oregon tried to influence voter turnout, and thereby the results of a local election, by sprinkling salmonella bacteria onto salad bars of several restaurants. Although more than seven hundred fifty people became ill, the cult's plan failed. In 1987 a Christian supremacist group in Arkansas was discovered to have thirty gallons of cyanide poison. The group planned to poison the water supplies of several United States cities.

In 1995 an Ohio white supremacist who was a laboratory technician made a letterhead of a fictitious research lab and ordered several vials of the bacteria that causes bubonic plague from a Maryland biomedical supply center. The order was already en route when he called the center expressing impatience. His call prompted concern. Government agencies were contacted and the man later served a short jail sentence for fraud.

The Maryland biomedical firm American Type Culture Collection is a nonprofit research group that supplies samples of germs for medical research and other legitimate purposes. It is only one of about fifteen hundred germ banks in the world. The group maintains live collections of disease microbes that are vital for research in producing treatments, including vaccines, and for other medical uses. Botulinum toxin, for example, is used by dermatologists to help remove wrinkles. However, these germ banks have unwittingly supplied microbes to rogue nations and to terrorists. In the 1980s, American Type Culture Collection sent anthrax bacteria to Iraq, before that nation's germ warfare program became known.

In 1995 the United States government tightened the rules affecting the handling and distribution of deadly microbes at germ banks. However, this only affected United States germ banks. The rules in other countries vary considerably, so dangerous materials from germ banks might still reach a nation or terrorist group seeking bioweapons. People knowledgeable about deadly germs can also find them in nature. For example, they can collect anthrax spores when this disease strikes cattle or other livestock.

Germ Scientists for Hire

The breakup of the Soviet Union added another worrisome factor to concerns about biological weapons.

Thousands of scientists had been employed in the Soviet's massive germ warfare program. By the mid-1990s, however, many were out of work. Research centers struggled to change to peacetime subjects (making pesticides, for example), but there was little money for equipment. Salaries were cut.

In 1998 Russian scientists reported that several researchers had been lured to work on biological weapons for Iran. Others had agreed to conduct research for Iran while remaining in Russia. They were well paid in a time of Russian economic chaos. The situation was ripe for other nations or even terrorist groups to recruit experts in germ warfare.

The United States took steps to compete. It did not hire Russian scientists but offered them such incentives as joint research projects and financial help in converting former germ warfare laboratories to civilian use. In 1998 United States senator Richard Lugar said, "This is a high-stakes game to win the hearts and minds of Russia's best scientists, who are dangerous simply because of what they know."

The United States also has committed up to $6 million to strengthen the security against theft or diversion of germs from Vector, a Russian germ bank. Vector maintains several strains of smallpox— a deadly disease that has been wiped out in the human population but still exists in germ banks. Furthermore, the United States persuaded Japan and Europe to help finance a research center in Moscow that aims to find peacetime work for former Soviet weapons scientists.

How Real Is the Bioterrorism Threat?

According to a 1993 Congressional study, it would take only one hundred kilograms of dried anthrax spores, spread by a low-flying aircraft over a city on a cool, calm night, to cause between 1 million and 3 million deaths.

However, germ weapons have never played a major role in war or in terrorism, and some experts say their danger is exaggerated. Biological weapons are more difficult to use and have less predictable results than chemical or conventional arms. The best bioweapon efforts of Japan's Aum Shinrikyo cult failed to cause any deaths. Speaking of biological weapons, Dr. Norton Zindler, a biologist at Rockefeller University, said, "They scare people but they're ineffective as weapons and that is a major reason why they have not been used."

Some worries about germ weapons are unrealistic. One fear is that a city's supply of drinking water could be poisoned or contaminated with a disease.

According to William Patrick, an antiterrorist expert who helped develop germ weapons for the United States government, "Municipal water supplies are very difficult to contaminate." In 1998, he explained that "dilution and diffusion factors as well as chlorination" of water would weaken a chemical or biological assault.

On the other hand, some who study terrorism believe this form of warfare will definitely occur—and do damage. Mr. Patrick believes that terrorist attacks with germs are inevitable. "It scares me. It's just a matter of time. It's not *if*. It's *when*."

New Kind of Terrorists?

Some experts believe that a new type of terrorist group has emerged. Traditional groups, such as the Irish Republican Army, usually do not kill people indiscriminately. They have political goals to meet and do not want to lose the sympathy of their civilian supporters. In contrast, Japan's Aum Shinrikyo cult aimed to kill nearly everyone on Earth. There seem to be growing numbers of groups that do not see themselves as part of a system worth saving but as outsiders. They seek vast changes and seem willing to kill millions of people to put the world on the right track.

In 1998 Brad Roberts, chairman of the Research Advisory Council of the Chemical and Biological Arms Control Institute, said of this new breed of terrorist, "Today, organizations exist that advocate the use of violence not in order to gain some political concession or piece of territory but solely for the purpose of extortion, revenge, racial hatred, or God's mandate. Some see mass murder as a calling from God."

Kyle Olson, an expert on cults and chemical weapons at Research Planning, said, "These days, we have cults and groups that think of themselves as the right minority against the majority." They are willing to take extraordinary steps for what they believe is the good of their group or of humanity. These steps,

Olson added, can be an attempt to "exterminate people that they consider their inferiors or people who are hostile to them."

Many experts on biological and chemical arms think that terrorists are much more likely to use such weapons than are nations. A country's leaders would think very carefully about using these weapons of mass destruction. The punishment from other nations could be devastating. A terrorist group, in contrast, might believe it could get away with it.

Preparing for Germ Attacks

In the 1990s the United States took steps to prepare for germ or chemical attacks, abroad or at home. One action, begun in 1997, was to vaccinate all 2.4 million members of the armed forces against anthrax. (The vaccination program was scheduled to be complete in 2004.) This was aimed at protecting the forces in case they were attacked with anthrax spores during some military action. Some members of the armed forces suspected a link between the anthrax vaccine and Gulf War Syndrome and refused the anthrax shots. They were demoted or discharged from military service.

Some biological weapons experts pointed out a serious flaw in the military vaccination program: The vaccine used does not give protection against all strains of anthrax. Soviet scientists developed a variety of anthrax that was not affected by the vaccine. Knowledge about the United States' vaccine could be seen by another nation or by a terrorist group as a weakness to be exploited. Conrad Istock, a Cornell University biologist and expert on bioweapons, wrote in 1998, "The anthrax vaccination program is a very bad idea. . . . The program will encourage and intensify several 'biological arms races.' It will also create new incentives for the manufacture and use of a wide variety of biological weapons. And it tells the world that the United States *expects* anthrax to be used in war, thereby eroding the force of the Biological and Toxin Weapons Convention."

The U.S. Department of Defense also began stockpiling vaccines against several diseases, including smallpox. And the United States government began storing vaccines and other medicines to help protect its citizens, especially police, fire, and health workers. All existing supplies of anthrax vaccine were being used by the armed forces, so there were none for civilian use. The earliest that a new variety of anthrax vaccine would be available for either military or civilian use would be 2005.

Beginning in 1996 the Domestic Preparedness Program trained emergency workers in one hundred twenty United States cities to respond to biological, chemical, or nuclear terrorism. This program was to be complete in 2001. Even as it proceeded, however, it was sharply criticized by medical experts. One of the most influential critics was Donald A. Henderson of the Johns Hopkins Center for Civilian Biodefense Studies.

In 1998 Dr. Henderson wrote, "Virtually all federal efforts in strategic planning and training have so far been directed toward crisis management after a chemical release or an explosion." And that, he wrote, does not prepare the country for a germ attack, since

> the expected scenario after release of a biological agent is entirely different. The release would be silent and would almost certainly be undetected. The cloud would be invisible, odorless, and tasteless. . . . No one would know until days or weeks later that anyone had been infected (depending on the microbe). Then patients would begin appearing in emergency rooms and physicians' offices with symptoms of a strange disease that few physicians had ever seen.

Thus the first responders to a biological weapon attack would not be police or fire departments but doctors, nurses, and other health care workers who are woefully unprepared. Dr. Henderson and others urged that emergency room workers be taught to recognize symptoms of a germ attack, especially of anthrax and smallpox. In a real germ attack, quick and accurate laboratory testing and identification of microbes would also be vital. Supplies of vaccines must be greatly increased; cities and states must make plans for managing a potential epidemic affecting many thousands of people.

Some skeptics continue to believe that there is little risk of a successful germ attack. As Japan's Aum Shinrikyo cult learned, grand plans can be difficult to carry out. However, this cult's failures can be studied and corrected by other terrorist groups. After all, it has taken years for nuclear weapons and other weapons of mass destruction to be detonated with any success. The challenge of effectively spreading large amounts of a deadly disease may still be met.

The threat of bioterrorism is real. At the dawn of the twenty-first century it seemed likely to pose a more serious threat than nuclear war. It is wise to take extraordinary steps to keep deadly germs out of the hands of terrorists and to prepare for the worst should these steps fail.

7

Controlling the Cruelest Weapons

Any progress toward reducing the threat of chemical warfare has to include the destruction of existing arsenals. A significant step was taken in 1990 when the United States and the Soviet Union agreed on a plan to slash their stores of poison gas.

The goal of each country was to destroy most of the stocks of chemical weapons within a few years. Unfortunately, getting rid of chemical arms is difficult and costly (often more expensive than making them). The Soviet program, in particular, ran into troubles after that nation broke apart. Most of the chemical

86

arms were stored in Russia—forty thousand tons of nerve gas and mustard gas at seven sites. Even with economic and technical help from the United States, Russia made slow progress and seemed unlikely to destroy its chemical arms by its deadline of 2007. An expensive incineration plant for burning chemical arms had to be built at each of the seven storage sites, and the plants themselves can take several years to build.

Destruction of the smaller United States arsenal—thirty thousand tons—began in 1993 at Johnson Atoll, which lies about eight hundred miles from Hawaii. About two hundred eighty thousand chemical weapons withdrawn from Europe had been stored on the island. By 2002, all will have been burned, and the incinerator and other facilities dismantled.

In 1996, incineration of chemical arms began on the United States mainland, at the Tooele Army Depot in Utah, where 44 percent of United States chemical weapons were stored. Some environmentalists and local residents protested but the incinerator operated without incident and steadily reduced stocks of bombs, rockets, and bulk containers of poison gases. Meanwhile, similar incinerators were being built at other chemical arms depots in Alabama, Arkansas, and Oregon. The United States seems likely to meet a 2004 deadline for destruction of its chemical arms.

Steps Toward a Chemical Weapons Treaty

Chemical disarmament by two major world powers was a hopeful sign, but only a tiny step. An arms

In Iraq, United Nations inspectors destroyed a building and equipment that had been used to make missile fuel.

control conference, held in Paris in 1989, resulted in 149 countries calling for "a global and comprehensive and effectively verifiable" chemical weapons treaty to be reached at an early date. Behind these noble words, however, remained major obstacles to such a treaty. Concerned about Israel's nuclear weapons, Arab nations tried to link chemical disarmament to nuclear disarmament.

At the 1989 chemical arms control conference, the United States opposed efforts to censure Iraq and Libya for their chemical attacks on neighbors. (This stance was an inducement for these countries to attend, which they did.) A year later intelligence reports revealed that Libya had resumed making chemical weapons. These events underscored the need for international agreement on getting tough with those who use such weapons and on restricting the sale of materials that can be used to make chemical arms.

Ingredients for Chemical Weapons

Many of the raw materials used to make chemical arms are fairly harmless and common until processed. Thiodigylcol, for example, has many uses. It is used to make ink for ballpoint pens and in finishing textiles. When it is mixed with hydrochloric acid, however, the product is mustard.

Thiodigylcol is one of nine chemicals closely linked to the manufacture of chemical weapons. Trade in these nine chemicals needs to be carefully controlled. About fifty other chemicals are often used in producing chemical arms, so their sale should be monitored, too. For trade restrictions to work, however, all nations that export chemicals must cooperate.

A 1990 study listed 201 companies in twenty-one countries from which Iraq acquired the chemicals and equipment it needed to make chemical weapons. Many of the companies were in West Germany; eighteen were in the United States. A group of Western nations, including the United States, tightened their export rules, agreeing to closely monitor and restrict sales of chemicals and equipment

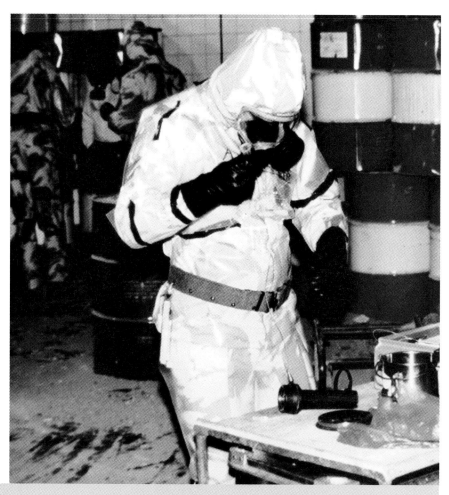

Some chemicals that have harmless peacetime uses can also be key ingredients of chemical weapons. Chlorine is one chemical that acts both ways.

United Nations inspectors tried to monitor activities at this chlorine production plant in Iraq. The poster in front of the plant is of Iraqi leader Saddam Hussein.

needed for making poison gases. As a result, Iraq, Iran, and other Middle Eastern nations began to obtain needed chemicals from India. The Western nations pressed India to stop such trade. Instead, India called for a worldwide ban on chemical weapons.

In 1992 this ban was agreed to by negotiators from thirty-eight nations. They completed a landmark agreement—the Chemical Weapons Convention.

Steps Toward a Chemical Arms Treaty

By 1999, 123 nations had signed the Chemical Weapons Convention. This arms control treaty was dramatically different from the Biological and Toxin Weapons Convention. The latter was just five pages long, the former 186 pages long. The difference was that the biological arms treaty had no system for verifying whether nations were cooperating. The chemical arms treaty did, partly because the biological arms treaty was ineffective without verification. It had been called a "dog without teeth."

Any nations that agreed to the terms of the chemical arms treaty were required to give detailed accounts of current and past shipments of equipment and chemical ingredients that could be used to make chemical weapons. An international agency, the Organization for the Prohibition of Chemical Weapons, was established to gather this information and to enforce the Chemical Weapons Convention. Under the terms of the treaty, a country accused of having a chemical weapons program must allow inspections and a thorough investigation. If the country refuses to cooperate, it will face tough sanctions— political, economic, and perhaps military. Under the treaty, neighboring nations can ask for international help to protect their citizens. This feature, it is hoped, will reduce the need for such nations to develop their own chemical arms to match their neighbor's arsenal.

Working to Control All of the Cruelest Weapons

Late in the twentieth century, negotiators from many nations met repeatedly in Geneva, Switzerland, and

Chemical arms are stored in dozens of these shelters in Utah. Getting rid of chemical arms safely costs more than it does to create such weapons.

made progress toward a plan to enforce the Biological and Toxin Weapons Convention. The basic plan was that certain facilities in a nation would declare which potential germ warfare microbes they possessed. They could be inspected to check the truthfulness of their declarations. They could be thoroughly investigated if a treaty violation was suspected. The investigation could include short-notice "challenge inspections," that are a key part of the Chemical Weapons Convention. Countries trying to run a secret biological weapons program would eventually be discovered and punished by the United Nations. The threat of punishment, it was hoped, would cause some nations to decide that a biological warfare program was too risky to start or to continue.

This verification and enforcement of the treaty worried the biotechnology and pharmaceutical industries worldwide. Part of a company's success often depends on keeping details about its production secret. Industrial spying does occur. However, industries in the United States and Europe began to accept the idea that some inspections and investigations would be needed in order to finally enforce the treaty against biological weapons.

Neither the chemical arms treaty nor biological arms treaty was foolproof. However, having a verification program for both, and the threat that violators could be severely punished, raised hopes that an arms race with these weapons could be avoided.

In his book *The Eleventh Plague*, Rutgers University professor Leonard A. Cole wrote of chemical and biological arms: "The longer these weapons are around, the more their sense of illegitimacy erodes, and the more likely they will be used—by armies and by terrorists."

Tough enforcement of the treaties against chemical and biological weapons might stop erosion of their illegitimacy. It might reinforce the idea that using such weapons is immoral. A British chemist, Julian Perry Robinson, asked if there was not "a perception widespread throughout different civilizations that fighting with poison is somehow reprehensible, immoral, utterly wrong . . . ?"

Reawakening this view could help protect people everywhere from humankind's cruelest weapons.

Appendix

Chemical and Biological Arms

Listed on the next three pages are the chemical and biological weapons that have been used in war and many others that have been studied for that purpose. More complete lists appear in the appendixes of *Gene Wars: Military Control Over the New Genetic Technologies* and *Preventing a Biological Arms Race* (see "Further Reading").

Chemical Weapons

Tear gases: CAP (CN), CS, and Adamsite (DM). Also called harassing agents, irritant agents, or incapacitants, these substances act rapidly and can cause a short-term flow of tears, an itching or burning feeling in the skin, coughing, sneezing, and vomiting.

Choking gases: Chlorine, Phosgene, and Chloropicrin. Once inhaled, these gases inflame lung tissues, causing fluids to build up, leading to bronchitis, pneumonia, and sometimes death, as the victim drowns from within.

Blistering agents: Mustards (sulfur or nitrogen) and Lewisite. Also called vesicants, blistering agents attack the skin and eyes, causing burns, blisters, and blindness that can last a week or more. Inhaling high concentrations can be lethal.

Blood agents: Hydrogen cyanide and Cyanogen chloride. Blood agents act by destroying an enzyme in red blood cells needed for oxygen to be released to body tissues. Low doses cause headache, nausea, and fatigue. High doses cause rapid breathing, paralysis, and convulsions.

Nerve agents: Tabun, Sarin, Soman, and VX. Nerve agents act by breaking down an enzyme needed where nerves relay signals to muscles. Without the enzyme, muscles contract wildly. Low doses cause sweating and tremors. High doses cause breathing difficulty, nausea, cramps, twitching, involuntary defecation, staggering, coma, and convulsion. Inhaling a large dose can cause death in a few minutes.

Possible Biological Weapons

Diseases caused by viruses:

Dengue fever	Lassa fever
Ebola fever	Rift Valley fever
Equine encephalitis	Smallpox
Influenza	Yellow fever

Diseases caused by bacteria:

Anthrax	Plague
Cholera	Tetanus
Dysentery	Tularemia
Glanders	Typhoid
Legionnaires' Disease	

Disease caused by rickettsiae:
Q-fever

Natural toxins and their sources:

Toxin	Source
Aflatoxin	fungus
Batrachotoxin	Columbian frog
Botulin	bacterium
Cobrotoxin	Chinese cobra
Crotoxin	South American rattlesnake
Coral toxins	corals
Ricin	castor bean plant
Saxitoxin	shellfish
Sea wasp toxin	jellyfish
Staphyloccus	bacterium
Tetanus toxin	bacterium

Chemical Weapons Convention

Excerpted from the *Fact Sheet* of September 1998, published by the United States Arms Control and Disarmament Agency, Washington, D.C.:

The Chemical Weapons Convention (CWC) is a global treaty that bans an entire class of weapons of mass destruction: chemical weapons. The CWC bans the production, acquisition, stockpiling, transfer, and use of chemical weapons. It entered into force April 29, 1997.

Chemical weapons pose a threat not just to our military but to innocent civilians, as the 1995 poison gas attack in the Japanese subway showed. Certain aspects of the CWC, including its law enforcement requirements and nonproliferation provisions, strengthen existing efforts to fight chemical terrorism. The CWC is a central element of United States arms control and nonproliferation policy that strengthens United States national security and contributes to global stability.

Under the CWC, each State Party undertakes never, under any circumstances, to:

- develop, produce, otherwise acquire, stockpile, or retain chemical weapons, or transfer, directly or indirectly, chemical weapons to anyone;
- use chemical weapons;
- engage in any military preparation to use chemical weapons; and
- assist, encourage, or induce, in any way, anyone to engage in any activity prohibited to a State Party under this Convention.

In addition, each State Party undertakes, all in accordance with the provisions of the Convention, to:
- destroy the chemical weapons it owns or possesses or that are located in any place under its jurisdiction or control;
- destroy all chemical weapons it abandoned on the territory of another State Party; and
- destroy any chemical weapons production facilities it owns or possesses or that are located in any place under its jurisdiction or control.

Today, we suspect some twenty countries have or may be developing chemical weapons. These weapons are attractive to countries or individuals seeking a mass-destruction capability because they are relatively cheap to produce and do not demand the elaborate technical infrastructure needed to make nuclear weapons. It is therefore all the more vital to establish an international bulwark against the acquisition and use of these weapons.

The CWC is the most ambitious treaty in the

history of arms control. Whereas most arms control treaties in the past have only limited weapons, the CWC requires their outright elimination. Parties to the Convention must destroy any and all chemical weapons and chemical weapons production facilities.

The Chemical Weapons Convention and Industry

The CWC is the first arms control treaty to widely affect the private sector. Although the United States does not manufacture chemical weapons, it does produce, process, and consume a number of chemicals that can be used to produce chemical weapons. For example, a solvent used in ballpoint pen ink can be easily converted into mustard gas, and a chemical involved in the production of fire retardants and pesticides can be used to make nerve agents. Thus, any treaty to ban chemical weapons must monitor commercial facilities that produce, process, or consume dual-use chemicals to ensure they are not diverted for prohibited purposes.

The CWC provisions covering chemical facilities were developed with the active participation of industry representatives. The verification regime is intrusive enough to build confidence that member states are complying with the treaty, yet it respects industry's legitimate interests in safeguarding proprietary information and avoiding disruption of production.

The CWC and the Military

The CWC specifically allows parties to maintain chemical weapons defensive programs and does not constrain non-chemical weapon (CW) military responses to a chemical weapons attack. John Shalikashvili, former chairman of the Joint Chiefs of Staff, has said in Senate testimony, "Desert Storm proved that retaliation in kind is not required to deter the use of chemical weapons." He explained, "the U.S. military's ability to deter chemical weapons in a post-CW world will be predicated upon a robust chemical weapons defense capability, and the ability to rapidly bring to bear superior and over-whelming military force in retaliation against a chemical attack." As Defense Secretary Cheney said during the Gulf War, and as former defense secretary Perry reiterated that the U.S. response to a chemical weapons attack would be absolutely overwhelming and devastating.

CWC Implementation

With or without the CWC, the United States is already destroying its chemical weapons in accordance with a law Congress passed more than a decade ago requiring destruction of the bulk of the U.S. chemical weapons stockpile. That process is under way, with completion slated by the end of 2004. The CWC now requires all State Parties that possess chemical weapons to destroy their stockpiles by 2007.

The U.S. is a member of the Executive Council of the Organization for the Prohibition of Chemical Weapons, in The Hague, that will oversee implementation of the CWC. U.S. citizens serve as international inspectors and in other key positions relating to verification of the treaty. In the United States, the Department of Commerce expects to publish the regulations pertaining to CWC verification after enactment of the CWC Implementation Act.

The CWC puts into place a legally binding international standard outlawing the acquisition and possession, as well as use, of chemical weapons. The Convention not only requires State Parties to destroy their chemical weapons arsenals but prohibits them from transferring chemical weapons to other countries or assisting anyone in prohibited activities. Combined with restrictions on chemical trade in CWC-controlled chemicals with nonparties, these provisions increase the costs and difficulties of acquiring chemical weapons for states that choose not to participate.

Universal adherence and complete abolition of chemical weapons won't be achieved immediately. But the Convention slows and even reverses chemical weapons proliferation by isolating the small number of rogue states that refuse to join the regime, limiting their access to precursor chemicals, and bringing international political and economic pressures to bear if such states continue their chemical weapons programs.

Further Reading

Berstein, Barton. "The Birth of the U.S. Biological-Warfare Program." *Scientific American*, June 1987, pp. 116–121.

Blumenthal, Ralph. "Japanese Germ-War Atrocities: A Half-Century of Stonewalling the World." *The New York Times*, March 4, 1999, p. A12.

Broad, William. "How Japan Germ Terror Alerted World." *The New York Times*, May 26, 1998, pp. 1, 10.

Cecil, Paul. *Herbicidal Warfare: The RANCH HAND Project in Vietnam*. New York: Praeger, 1986.

Cipkowski, Peter. *Understanding the Crisis in the Persian Gulf*. New York: John Wiley & Sons, Inc., 1991.

Cole, Leonard. *Clouds of Secrecy: The Army's Germ Warfare Tests Over Populated Areas*. Totowa, N.J.: Rowman & Littlefield, 1988.

Cole, Leonard. *The Eleventh Plague: The Politics of Biological and Chemical Warfare*. New York: W. H. Freeman, 1996.

Flowerree, Charles, and Gordon Burck. *International Handbook on Chemical Weapons Proliferation*. Westport, Conn.: Greenwood Press, 1991.

Geissler, Erhard, ed. *Biological and Toxin Weapons Today*. New York: Oxford University Press, 1986.

Haber, Ludwig. *The Poisonous Cloud: Chemical Warfare in the First World War*. New York: Oxford University Press, 1986.

Henderson, Donald. "The Looming Threat of Bioterrorism." *Science*, February 26, 1999, pp. 1279–1282.

Hogendorn, E. J. "A Chemical Weapons Atlas." *Bulletin of the Atomic Scientists*, September–October 1997, pp. 35–39.

Istock, Conrad. "Bad Medicine." *Bulletin of the Atomic Scientists*, November–December 1998, pp. 21–23.

King, Jonathan. "The Threat of Biological Weapons." *Technology Review*, May–June 1982, pp. 10–11.

Landau, Elaine. *Chemical and Biological Warfare*. New York: Dutton, 1991.

MacRae-Campbell, Linda and Micki McKisson. *War: The Global Battlefield*. Galeburg, Ill., 1990.

Marshall, Eliot. "Iraq's Chemical Warfare: Case Proved." *Science*, April 13, 1984, pp. 130–132.

Meselson, Matthew. "The Myth of Chemical Superweapons." *Bulletin of the Atomic Scientists*, April 1991, pp. 12–15.

O'Connell, Robert. *Of Arms and Men: A History of War, Weapons, and Aggression*. New York: Oxford University Press, 1989.

Piller, Charles, and Keith Yamamoto. *Gene Wars: Military Control Over the New Genetic Technologies*. New York: William Morrow, 1988. (The appendixes of this book include tables of biological and chemical weapons, and texts of the treaties aimed at controlling them.)

Robinson, Julian, J. Guillemin, and M. Meselson. "Yellow Rain: The Story Collapses." *Foreign Policy*, Fall 1987, pp. 100–117. (An updated version of this article appears on pp. 220–235 of *Preventing a Biological Arms Race*, cited below.)

Rogers, Paul, Simon Whitby, and Malcolm Dando. "Biological Warfare Against Crops." *Scientific American*, June 1999, pp. 70–75.

Rose, Steven. "Biotechnology at War." *New Scientist*, March 19, 1987, pp. 33–37.

Seeley, Thomas, et al. "Yellow Rain." *Scientific American*, September 1985, pp. 128–137.

Spiers, Edward. *Chemical Weaponry: A Continuing Challenge*. New York: St. Martin's Press, 1989.

Taylor, L. B., Jr., and C. L. Taylor. *Chemical & Biological Warfare*. Danbury, Conn.: Franklin Watts Inc., 1992.

United Nations General Assembly. *Report of the Secretary-General on Chemical and Bacteriological (Biological) Weapons and the Effects of Their Possible Use*. New York: United Nations, 1969.

Vasilakis, Anastasia. "The Gulf War Within." *Discover*, August 1997, pp. 69–75.

Vegar, Jose. "Terrorism's New Breed." *Bulletin of the Atomic Scientists*, March–April 1998, pp. 50–55.

Warry, John. *Warfare in the Classical World*. New York: St. Martin's Press, 1980.

Whiteside, Thomas. "The Yellow-Rain Complex." *The New Yorker*, February 11, 1991, pp. 38–67, and February 18, 1991, pp. 44–68.

Wright, Susan, ed. *Preventing a Biological Arms Race*. Cambridge, Mass.: MIT Press, 1990.

Internet Addresses

The Chemical and Biological Warfare Project
<http://www.sipri.se/cbw/cbw-mainpage.html>
Gives information on the work being done on prevention at the Stockholm International Peace Research Institute.

Chemical Warfare Agents
<http://www.opcw.nl/chemhaz/cwagents.htm>
An overview of chemicals defined as chemical weapons.

Background on Chemical Warfare
<http://www.mitretek.org/mission/envene/chemical/
    chem_back.html>
Reference material that explains the chemistry and toxicity of chemical warfare agents, and discusses chemical weapons and countermeasures. Also addresses issues related to the impact of chemical weapons on society and attempts to control that impact.

Medical Aspects of Chemical and Biological Warfare
<http://www.nbcmed.org/SiteContent/HomePage/
    WhatsNew>
A table of contents that links to information on the medical aspects of chemical and biological warfare, put out by the United States Army.

Index

About the Author

Laurence Pringle earned degrees in wildlife conservation and was an editor of a children's science magazine before becoming a freelance writer in 1970. He is the author of more than ninety nonfiction books for young people. Pringle has won many awards, including the 1999 Washington Post/Children's Book Guild Nonfiction Award for his body of work.